Where Is Your Part of Fortune?

by

Barbara Goldsmith

Where Is Your Part of Fortune?

Copyright © 2018
Barbara Goldsmith. All Rights Reserved

First Edition 2018

ISBN: 978-1-72-416230-4

This book is copyright protected. Except for the purpose of reviewing, no part of this publication may be reproduced or transmitted in any form or by any means, electronic or mechanical, including photocopying, recording or any information storage or retrieval system, without prior permission in writing from the publisher.

Other Titles by Barbara Goldsmith

Astrology Made Easy - A Handy Reference Guide
The Elements - Physical and Metaphysical Astrology
Moon Cycles

CONTENTS

Chapter One
What is the Part of Fortune?

Chapter Two
Part of Fortune in the Twelve Houses

Chapter Three
Part of Fortune in the Twelve Signs

Chapter Four
Aspects to the Part of Fortune

Chapter Five
Famous People's Part of Fortune

Chapter Six
Part of Fortune from a Soul Perspective

Where Is Your Part of Fortune?

CHAPTER ONE

WHAT IS THE PART OF FORTUNE?

You won't find a great deal of information out there about the Part of Fortune, so I decided to write a short book outlining what it is and how to interpret it in your own chart.

Modern astrology tends to regard the Part of Fortune as a minor point, but this was not the case with ancient astrology.

As the Part of Fortune is derived from the Sun, Moon and Ascendant, which are three of the most significant places in a chart, it could be said that the Part of Fortune is just as important as all three put together.

Where Is Your Part of Fortune?

The more I delve into and research this fascinating Part, the more I find that it reveals about your prosperity, your career path, your mode of income, your body and health, your connection with your outside world, and, on a deeper level, how your soul can grow into its highest expression.

Keep in mind that, while the Part of Fortune is a valuable point, it must eventually be synthesised with the entire chart. For example, if the Part of Fortune shows healthy and good relationships, it is still important to examine the fifth, seventh and eleventh houses and their rulers and aspects to them to get the full picture.

HOW TO CALCULATE YOUR PART OF FORTUNE

If the Sun is in the first to sixth houses, then you are considered a night or nocturnal chart. If the Sun is in the seventh to twelfth houses, then you are a day or diurnal chart.

Barbara Goldsmith

The Part of Fortune is calculated as follows:

For day charts: Ascendant + Moon - Sun
For night charts: Ascendant + Sun - Moon

The above formulae should be measured by computing the longitudes of the Ascendant, Sun and Moon, as measured from 0 degrees Aries.

– It is done according to this table –

Aries	Add 0	Libra	Add 180
Taurus	Add 30	Scorpio	Add 210
Gemini	Add 60	Sagittarius	Add 240
Cancer	Add 90	Capricorn	Add 270
Leo	Add 120	Aquarius	Add 300
Virgo	Add 150	Pisces	Add 330

For example, take someone who has an Ascendant at 23 degrees Aries, a Sun at 22 degrees Leo and a Moon at 14 degrees Leo. As the Sun is between the Ascendant and the

Where Is Your Part of Fortune?

Descendant, this is a night birth, so you would use the night birth formula:

Ascendant + Sun - Moon
Ascendant 23 Aries is +23
Sun 29 Leo is +149
Moon 14 Leo is +134
Part of Fortune is: 23 + 149 - 134 = 38
Therefore, Part of Fortune is at 8 degrees Taurus.

As another example, take someone with an Ascendant at 25 degrees Libra, a Sun at 3 degrees Cancer, and a Moon at 0 degrees Capricorn. As the Sun is above the horizon, this is a day birth, so you would use the day birth formula:

Ascendant + Moon - Sun
Ascendant 25 Libra is +205
Moon 0 Capricorn is +270
Sun 3 Cancer is +93
Part of Fortune is: 205 + 270 - 93 = 382
As it is over 360 degrees, subtract 360 from 382 = 22
Therefore, Part of Fortune is at 22 degrees Aries.

For over a thousand years, the diurnal or day Part of Fortune has been the one that has been used by astrologers, and it still is to this day. This is because Ptolemy, an ancient authority, seemed to advocate doing all charts using the day formula. However, new translations of Ptolemy seem to indicate that this was not his intention. Most other ancient sources advocated using the day formula for day births and the night formula for night births.

In my experience, however, both the diurnal and the nocturnal placements of your Part of Fortune have relevance, so it is a good idea to draw up both so that you can learn more about the way in which you can interpret both these powerful points in your chart.

If you have a copy of your natal chart, the symbol of your diurnal Part of Fortune looks like a circle with an x inside it. The house in which it appears in your chart will show you where you are likely

Where Is Your Part of Fortune?

to have good fortune. It can represent physical, emotional, financial, intellectual or spiritual good luck.

It can indicate your best career direction or vocation and will show where your innate abilities and talents lie. It's where you feel most at home and most fulfilled. Astrologers sometimes call it your 'ray of hope' or your 'pot of gold'.

As the Part of Fortune is the balance point between your Ascendant, Sun and Moon, it has a very mystical quality. You can view it both from the mundane level and the spiritual or metaphysical level. It is important to remember that it does not operate like a planet, which represents an energetic force. Instead, it is something we have invented and represents a suggestion rather than something concrete and specific.

The pleasure you will derive from your Part of

Fortune will depend largely on how well you tune into the different energies of your Sun, Moon and Ascendant. If these three are working in harmony, the Part of Fortune will have a positive effect in your life. If not, it may bring you challenging experiences until you learn how to best balance these energies inside you.

Let's look at the meanings of these three key points in your chart.

The Sun is your core self, your vital force and your unique identity. Think about the sun generally. On a lovely sunny day, you feel brighter, more alive and more cheerful. On a dull, rainy, cloudy and overcast day, you may feel blue and more depressed.

It is very important to take care of the Sun in your chart so that you feel bright and alive. If you are not taking care of your Sun, you'll probably have the blues.

Where Is Your Part of Fortune?

A key phrase about the Sun is: 'To thine own self be true.'

It's about being authentic and real, and acting with integrity.

If you are doing this, you are expressing the true nature of the Sun in your chart.

With twelve different Sun signs and twelve houses, there are many ways in which the Sun can be emphasised in an astrology chart. However, its innate essence is the same: it is your identity and your vitality.

The Moon is your emotional nature, your habitual patterns and knee-jerk reactions to the events you experience in your life.

How well you can take care of your Moon will indicate the degree of happiness you feel. It is connected to the heart and to the mother.

Barbara Goldsmith

When you were young, if you had a loving mother who comforted you and who nurtured you, then you probably have a positive way of nurturing yourself.

For example, if one day you are not feeling well, instead of pushing yourself to continue and to take care of all your responsibilities, you allow yourself to rest and you take care of yourself instead. This is a healthy way of taking care of your Moon.

If your mother was not very nurturing, didn't touch you and was cold-hearted, then the chances are that you don't know how to take care of yourself very well.

The Moon teaches you to do what is irrational but that which brings you joy. For example, if you enjoy playing the piano, or painting, or gardening, and, even though it may not make you a living, you still do it regardless, you are looking after your Moon energy. It's about not giving up those things that bring you joy.

The Ascendant describes how you look, your personality and how you present yourself to the world. A good way to explain it would be to say it represents your style. You might say this is superficial, and to a certain extent it is.

While the Ascendant often describes the way you look, it is a coloured filter through which the rest of the chart shines. It is extremely variable and has a multitude of meanings, depending on the placement of the other planets in your chart. It shows the place in your chart where great fortune and happiness can come to you, so long as you are authentic and act with integrity.

THE PLACEMENT OF YOUR PART OF FORTUNE

Although there are no hard and fast rules about

the placement of your Part of Fortune, it is considered favourably placed:

- In the second, fifth, eighth and eleventh houses
- In the angular houses, which are the first, fourth, seventh and tenth
- In Taurus or Libra – Venus-ruled signs
- Conjunct Venus or Jupiter
- Trine or sextile to Jupiter
- Conjunct the Sun
- Trine the ruler of the second house

IT IS CONSIDERED NOT QUITE AS WELL-PLACED

- In the cadent houses, which are the third, sixth, ninth and twelfth
- Square or opposite to Mars or Saturn
- When unaspected
- When it has a retrograde sign ruler

According to Robert Hand's research, the sign

Where Is Your Part of Fortune?

of the Part of Fortune and its ruler give good information on a profession that can make you money, along with your tenth house.

The tenth sign from the Part of Fortune is also very good for helping to describe the actual social role the occupation serves.

The eleventh sign from the Part of Fortune has a role in determining how well and by what means one earns money.

Its placement isn't only in a certain house and sign in your chart, but it can also make aspects to other planets and they too can give you pointers as to how to develop this good fortune in your life.

You will probably have strong reactions to people who have planets that make aspects to your Part of Fortune. For example, many of my closest friends have their Sun or their Moon conjunct my Part of Fortune. It is as if they can light up the things in my life that will make me happy. Once you are familiar with the placement of your Part of Fortune in your chart, you might be surprised to see how some of the important people in your life have planets that stimulate that point in your chart.

It is important to remember that the Part of Fortune is just one factor in your chart, so while the following descriptions I am going to give you about all the signs and houses that the Part of Fortune can be placed in will be useful, you will need to combine them with your understanding of the whole chart to gain a really deep knowledge of the dynamics at play.

CHAPTER TWO

PART OF FORTUNE IN THE TWELVE HOUSES

FIRST HOUSE PART OF FORTUNE

You were born at or just after a New Moon and, as a result, you have a strong personality. You need to stand out in your own unique way and you have a certain charm and magnetism. It's important for you to see the world through your own eyes rather than through other people's eyes. You must learn to focus your energy without getting distracted. Your greatest fortune comes when you are independent and self-sufficient. You have a competitive nature and it's best for you to compete with yourself and not with others. As you begin to master a more spiritual approach to your relationships with others, you will be able to experience the joy of self-fulfilment. On the mundane level, you may be involved with anything that improves how people look and feel. You might be a personal coach, mentor or trainer, a beauty therapist, a hair stylist or a counsellor. Anything involving personal enhancement or development would be a good field for you. You may have a very distinctive style of your own and you probably have an attractive or striking appearance. People will be attracted to your optimistic, upbeat energy.

Famous People with First House Part of Fortune

Madonna, Sean Connery, Prince William, Halle Berry, Tom Hanks, Kylie Minogue, Harrison Ford, Bob Dylan, Sarah Palin, Tiger Woods, Dustin Hoffman, Serena Williams.

SECOND HOUSE PART OF FORTUNE

You attain your good fortune by discovering what really matters to you. Money and possessions are only important in that they reflect your current values. You must be careful not to be attached to things that are no longer useful. You can be very lucky with money so long as what you are doing expresses your highest values. Friends may disappear from your life at times because of fundamental differences in your values. You need to learn how to stay true to your highest values. You will be able to teach the importance of living according to meaningful values and principles. You have an innate ability to attract money, possessions and assets to you. You will have a concern for financial security, but you don't really need to worry about it. You will have an ability to enjoy money and fine things. You probably like good food and anything that stimulates your senses, including body creams, lotions, perfumes, luxurious clothing and fabrics, works of art, music, colour, and anything that makes you feel good.

Famous People with Second House Part of Fortune

Barack Obama, Bob Geldof, Edgar Cayce, Richard Branson, Leonardo DiCaprio, Rihanna, Justin Timberlake, Jude Law, Oprah Winfrey, Clint Eastwood, Kevin Costner, Rod Stewart.

THIRD HOUSE PART OF FORTUNE

Communication in any form will bring you your greatest happiness. Your ability to think clearly and to use your mind will ultimately bring you your greatest luck. You will have a love of sharing your ideas as you are a natural teacher, trainer, mentor and coach. You have something very important to say in the world. You will have to watch out that you are not too critical. If you want others to be receptive to your ideas, you may have to curb your impatience, especially if their thinking skills are not as quick as yours. Your mind is so fast that other people sometimes cannot keep up with you, so you will have to find a way to communicate your ideas that is reachable for the average person. You have a unique ability to express your ideas in a way that helps people into greater understanding. You may have a great interest in different spiritual topics. You will probably like books, writing, talking, training, coaching, advising and being on the move. You will have a love of new experiences and of learning. This placement is often found in the charts of teachers, writers, speakers, trainers, journalists and those who express themselves with words.

Famous People with Third House Part of Fortune

Russell Crowe, Elizabeth Taylor, Nicholas Cage, Steven Spielberg, Warren Buffett, Yoko Ono,

Susan Sarandon, Venus Williams, Britney Spears, Anne Frank.

FOURTH HOUSE PART OF FORTUNE

You will gain a great sense of fulfilment from nurturing and giving. It's important for you to feel you are needed in some way. You need to build a strong emotional foundation in your life to support your future growth. You may have a keen interest in the earth, ecology, history, ancestry and how we can take care of our planet. You love nature and achieve deep satisfaction and happiness when you feel you are in alignment with all living things. This placement often brings blessings and luck to your home and family. Frequently, there is good fortune with real estate and land, especially in later life. You may become very wealthy in the latter part of your life. You need a sense of home to be happy and contented – not necessarily a mansion, but just somewhere that feels like home. You may have an interest in gardening, farming, growing vegetables or becoming self-sufficient. You want to have a nest – a safe place to live and to thrive. You may earn your living through property, real estate or a family business.

Famous People with Fourth House Part of Fortune

George Clooney, Cameron Diaz, Robbie Williams, J. F. Kennedy, Penélope Cruz, Eminem, George W. Bush, Roger Federer, George Harrison, Winona Ryder, Maria Shriver.

FIFTH HOUSE PART OF FORTUNE

Your greatest joy comes from being creative. You can make your dreams a reality. It's very important that you are discerning with your choice of friends and the people around you as they have the power to either inspire you or to pull you down. You are attracted to anything that involves self-expression, art, drama, dance, romance, children and music. You have a very strong will and can bring about anything you envision. There can be good luck with children and a talent in the arts and in design. Your gift is your ability to manifest your dreams. Your greatest happiness comes from putting your energy into whatever makes your heart sing. The joy you express is infectious and other people will be drawn to you. You may earn your living from artistic, creative and speculative activities and anything of an entrepreneurial nature. Success in your own business is likely with this placement.

Famous People with Fifth House Part of Fortune

Whitney Houston, Mel Gibson, Joan Baez, Antonio Banderas, Nelson Mandela, Drew Barrymore, Sophia Loren, Meg Ryan, Adele, Kim Kardashian.

Where Is Your Part of Fortune?

SIXTH HOUSE PART OF FORTUNE

You find happiness through work and through doing something you feel is useful and productive. You will be able to get along well with co-workers. You will have good fortune with your health as you are able to correct destructive habits and patterns that might undermine your health. You do well when you are supporting others and helping them to bring order into their lives. You are born just prior to a Full Moon and will have an interest in self-improvement and self-discipline. You want to improve other people's lives. You may excel in the field of health – for example, as a doctor, nurse, vet, naturopath, herbalist, physiotherapist, chiropractor, homeopath, healer, energy-worker or carer. You have an innate ability to help the underdog and you feel very happy when you can help someone less fortunate than you. You may have an interest in home improvement as well as improving health.

Famous People with Sixth House Part of Fortune

Shirley MacLaine, Eric Clapton, Roger Moore, Virginia Woolf, Ingrid Bergman, Martha Stewart, Julian Assange, Howard Stern, Liza Minnelli, Joe Biden.

SEVENTH HOUSE PART OF FORTUNE

You are born soon after a Full Moon and your greatest happiness comes through other people. You constantly seek interaction with others, possibly through marriage, friendship, partnerships and joint ventures. You feel happy when those around you are happy. You would do very well in a counselling, advising or mediating role. You like to soften people's problems and help them to find harmony in their lives. You need to ensure that you are not too easily influenced by others. Your good fortune and luck will always come through other people. They will

Where Is Your Part of Fortune?

either highlight your path to fortune or they will bring your fortune to you. You are very idealistic, and you want to only see the best in everyone. You shine in your relationships and you may have a relationship or partnership with someone who is very wealthy. A good career for you would be as a consultant, a therapist, a marriage counsellor or a social worker, or something in the legal profession, or any work that involves one-to-one relationships.

Famous People with Seventh House Part of Fortune

Paris Hilton, Bono, John Travolta, Édith Piaf, Coco Chanel, Leona Lewis, Luciano Pavarotti, Yves Saint Laurent, Susan Boyle, Christian Dior, John Cleese.

EIGHTH HOUSE PART OF FORTUNE

This placement brings helpful people into your

life who want to be of assistance to you. They want to protect you and nurture you. You need to constantly be aware of what you are holding onto and what you need to let go of. Recycling and giving away possessions from time to time is very beneficial for you. You experience joy when you release that which is no longer necessary. You are very good at advising people with their money and their assets. Your good fortune financially comes from assisting others. You want to protect them and, in turn, they are protective of you. Your greatest fortune comes through other people and you can have a very powerful influence on them. You are likely to be interested in the occult, spirituality, metaphysics, rejuvenation and regeneration. You have an attractive personal magnetism that draws people to you. You may earn your living through psychology, healing, surgery, investments, insurance business or managing other people's money and resources.

Where Is Your Part of Fortune?

FAMOUS PEOPLE WITH EIGHTH HOUSE PART OF FORTUNE

Princess Diana, Kurt Cobain, Bill Gates, Lady Gaga, Hillary Clinton, Vladimir Putin, Silvio Berlusconi, Prince Charles, Robin Williams, Jean-Paul Sartre.

NINTH HOUSE PART OF FORTUNE

Your good fortune and happiness come from learning and teaching what you have learnt. You have so much you want to teach and share with others. You have a gift for clairvoyance and for seeing into the future. This is a very good placement for international relations and business. This is a lucky position altogether and you will find and make your own luck. You will probably find success away from the place of your birth. You will always be broadening your horizons and you do well when working with global organisations and anything that involves equality and justice. You may earn your living through academic pursuits, travel, teaching, publishing, media or advertising. Travelling is likely to be a big part of your life. Foreigners and people from different cultures bring you good fortune.

Famous People with Ninth House Part of Fortune

Jennifer Lopez, John Lennon, Freddie Mercury, Bill Clinton, Cher, Ronald Reagan, Neil Armstrong, Paolo Coelho, Eva Perón, Neale Donald Walsch, John McEnroe, Albert Schweitzer.

TENTH HOUSE PART OF FORTUNE

The benefits of this placement don't necessarily fall into your lap, as they often have to be earnt through effort and hard work. You will have a strong sense of ethics and integrity. You can

Where Is Your Part of Fortune?

implement new structures in society that will be beneficial to the masses. You could be involved in politics or you may be active within your community, trying to create more equitable systems that will benefit everyone. You can achieve true success and public recognition in your field. You have a definite role to play in society. You are someone who can inspire others to be true to themselves and to see that, through hard work and discipline, you can achieve whatever you want. You are not afraid of hard work, but you are focused on achieving goals and gaining respect. Your good luck is derived from the respect you earn from being authentic without compromise. Once you have put the hard work in, your career can be very successful and enjoyable.

Famous People with Tenth House Part of Fortune

Albert Einstein, Vincent van Gogh, David Beckham, Frank Sinatra, Woody Allen,

Julio Iglesias, Ellen DeGeneres, Stephen King, Margaret Thatcher, Barbra Streisand, Christopher Reeve, Josh Groban.

ELEVENTH HOUSE PART OF FORTUNE

You have the gift of being able to draw people of like mind together. Good fortune comes to you from other people, especially your friends. You need contact with bright, intelligent people who stimulate your imagination. You are a dreamer and a visionary and can be a catalyst for change. You are way ahead of the times and you may often feel as though you don't belong where you are. You may be interested in astrology and it could give you valuable direction in the timing of events in your life. Your happiness comes from doing something that will benefit others, your community, or even humanity as a whole. You have an inventive mind and could come up with an innovative idea that could impact the world. Your greatest joy comes from experiencing

Where Is Your Part of Fortune?

your freedom and independence. There is an eccentric side to you that will not conform, and you feel joyful when you help others to access their individuality. Mental creativity comes easily to you.

Famous People with Eleventh House Part of Fortune

Angelina Jolie, Mahatma Gandhi, Helena Blavatsky, Steve Jobs, Pablo Picasso, Paul Newman, Elton John, Diana Ross, Aristotle Onassis, Stevie Wonder, J. R. R. Tolkien, Tony Robbins.

TWELFTH HOUSE PART OF FORTUNE

Your greatest joy comes from a feeling of alignment with your inner self. Silent periods of meditation and solitude are very important to you and show you a great deal. You have earnt many blessings from past lifetimes. This is an especially good placement for the healing profession. You have many invisible guides who are constantly helping you. Your psychic powers are great and your intuition is your best guide. You could do well in media, television, film, photography, music, or writing fiction and fantasy. You may be unaware of your good fortune. You have the gift of prophecy, spirituality and mysticism. You can dissolve your own karma. You may have a strong affinity with music and sound. Your greatest happiness is in the realisation that you are safe and at home wherever you are. You can go deeply into that which is hidden – into past lives to help others overcome obstacles in this lifetime that stem from destructive habit patterns from the past. Your earnings may be related to psychic work, medical research, prisons, hospitals, retreats, spiritual endeavours or anything in the metaphysical field.

Where Is Your Part of Fortune?

Famous People with Twelfth House Part of Fortune

Camilla, Duchess of Cornwall, Sting, Agatha Christie, Ringo Starr, Franz Kafka, Sylvia Plath, Annie Lennox, Émile Zola, Fred Astaire, Michel Gauquelin, Steve Wozniak.

CHAPTER THREE

PART OF FORTUNE IN THE TWELVE SIGNS

ARIES

You will have a great deal of energy and you need to be very active – not necessarily physically active, but maybe mentally active and alert. You are courageous, brave, confident and self-assured, and you love adventure and spontaneous expression. You may not have all these qualities right now, but these are the attributes that you can develop. You need to learn how to focus your energy effectively, and to be in control of your life. You are someone who derives great pleasure from taking initiative and you can achieve happiness and success through your innovative and creative efforts. You enjoy new challenges and overcoming obstacles. You can help and direct others towards more productive uses of their energy. You must be independent and not accept interference from others. Whatever you achieve will be through your own efforts and this brings you your greatest joy. Learn to trust your intuition.

Famous People

Marilyn Monroe, Charlie Chaplin, Napoleon Bonaparte, Justin Bieber, Nelson Mandela, Joan of Arc, Mike Tyson, Marlene Dietrich, Paramahansa Yogananda, Diego Maradona, Louis Pasteur.

TAURUS

You need to be productive and create tangible results for your efforts. You like peace and you can achieve contentment. This placement can bring good fortune with accumulating assets and possessions, so long as you are able to discern their value. Just collecting things for no reason will not bring you happiness. Whatever you gather must have value and meaning. You derive pleasure from building and sustaining new structures. You can be patient and achieve inner peace so long as you don't get too enmeshed in the mundane world of money and ownership. Your experience of joy is achieved when you produce real and lasting results from your efforts. You have a solidity within you that is very soothing for others, as they know they can depend on you. You get pleasure from being stable, persistent and practical. You may have a love of beauty, food, eating, nature and anything that stimulates your senses.

Famous People

Queen Elizabeth II, Victoria Beckham, Hugh Grant, Sophia Loren, Rudolf Steiner, Paula

Where Is Your Part of Fortune?

Abdul, Johann Wolfgang von Goethe, Warren Beatty, Sarah Ferguson, Julia Roberts.

GEMINI

You need to reach out to others and communicate, as you can bridge the gaps in understanding between people. As you use and develop your communication skills and your ability to learn, you will achieve success and joy. You might publish a bestseller or help others to get their work into the public domain. Those who live near you or work around you will always be there for you if you need them. You need to cultivate versatility, freedom of movement and your sense of humour. You are extremely curious, and you need to develop flexibility and the ability to go with the flow. You need to be fully engaged with everything that's going on around you without judging everything. Your happiness comes from being in the moment and sharing your exciting adventures with others. You love talking, anything that stimulates the mind, humour, play and developing your skills.

Famous People

Michelle Obama, Beyoncé Knowles-Carter, Meryl Streep, Jim Carrey, Olivia Newton-John, Steffi Graf, Gustave Flaubert, Michael Bublé, Barbara Walters, James Joyce.

CANCER

You seek security for yourself, but you can also help others find their security. You need to cultivate gentleness and caring. You have a great ability to nurture other people, animals, projects, creative endeavours, ideas and visions. Whatever it is, you can nurture something so that it becomes whole. This brings you your greatest happiness and joy. You can get in touch with the earth's energies and use them to make things grow and thrive. Try to develop the tenderness and caring qualities you have, and you will derive much enjoyment from nourishing all things so that they can flourish. You might have an interest in anything connected with the earth (e.g. gardening, growing food, protecting the land, animals and birds). You can empathise with the vulnerable and can teach them how to become self-reliant. You love home, family, memories, tradition, the past, food, nurturing, collecting things, music and real estate.

Famous People

Angela Merkel, Walt Disney, Leona Lewis, Hugo Chávez, Marcel Proust, Charles Dickens, Jane Austen, Charlotte Brontë, Plácido Domingo, Robert F. Kennedy.

LEO

With this placement, you need to cultivate recognition from others for your creativity to feel happy and successful. You are generous and optimistic and you can be a source of great inspiration. You are someone who leads by example and you are authentic. You give for the sheer joy of giving without any expectation of a return. You have an abundant creative energy that can bring about many new and exciting results. For you, great happiness comes from accomplishing large-scale achievements that inspire others to develop their creativity. You are a shining example of what a person can achieve. You can become a master in your field of expertise and this will bring you great joy. You love fun, drama, developing new businesses, games of any kind, art, sport, dance and anything creative.

Famous People

Brigitte Bardot, Bruce Willis, David Bowie, Celine Dion, Mick Jagger, Prince, Jimi Hendrix, Kevin Costner, Fidel Castro.

VIRGO

No matter what kind of health problem may be thrown at you, you will be able to find a solution to it. It doesn't mean that you can be over-confident with your health or abuse it, but, if you are sincere, you will be able to catch things before they become serious. You are able to study and to change destructive habit patterns so that you create a happier and more joyful life for yourself. You need to develop discrimination and logical analysis. You are happy when your environment is in order, as you are extremely sensitive to vibrations. This placement brings luck with your work, your career and your physical health. You may be drawn to the medical profession as a career or something that involves helping others. You enjoy feeling that you are making a valuable contribution and anything concerning wellness, health, nutrition, work, animals, volunteering and charity work would be fields in which you can excel.

Famous People

Mother Teresa, Michael Jackson, Jane Fonda, George Michael, Carlos Castaneda, Federico Fellini, Howard Hughes, Roman Polanski, Patrick Swayze.

LIBRA

You are happiest when you achieve balance in your relationships. You are probably a people pleaser and you will have to ensure that your needs are being met in your relationships and you are not making too many compromises. You try to cooperate with others, but this doesn't always work in your best interests. You need to discern the fine line between being helpful and giving too much. You experience joy when you feel as though you are part of something and that you belong. You have an innate ability to mediate successfully in both personal and professional relationships. Once you feel in harmony with the people around you and in your life, you experience your greatest fulfilment. You may have many lessons to learn about relationships before you truly achieve the balance you desire, but, once you have overcome these obstacles, your relationships bring great fulfilment and pleasure. You love discussions, one-to-one interactions, counselling, advising, coaching, training, harmony, diplomacy and elegance.

Famous People

Katy Perry, Michelle Pfeiffer, Penélope Cruz, Mel Gibson, Björk, Tom Hanks, Antonio Banderas, Kate Winslet, Nicholas Cage, Cary Grant.

SCORPIO

This is a very powerful placement and means you must act wisely and only with the best of intentions for everyone with whom you come into contact. You could be a powerful leader, singer, actor, spiritual teacher or mentor. You have the power to influence people positively or negatively. You have a keen perception and penetrating insight and you love to dive into the unknown and the unseen. Your happiness is achieved by getting to the core and bottom of situations. You are able to regenerate and rejuvenate yourself so that you can experience a rebirth and reinvent yourself. You will have the feeling that you have already 'died' many times this lifetime. You have wonderful recuperative powers that you can tap into whenever you desire. You are happiest when you can show people how to face their fears and go beyond them. You emanate confidence and assuredness. You love intensity, using personal power, empowering others, intimacy and deep soul connections.

Famous People

Tom Cruise, Elizabeth Hurley, Ludwig van

Where Is Your Part of Fortune?

Beethoven, J. K. Rowling, Lance Armstrong, Alice Bailey, Charles Darwin, Omar Sharif, Dane Rudhyar, George Gurdjieff.

SAGITTARIUS

Your success comes from exploring and reaching for new horizons and adventures. You seek truth and fairness and you may be interested in law or politics. This is a good position for a lawyer, judge or politician. You are not afraid to take risks and to try your luck because you will learn something from the experience. Your greatest fortune may lie far away from your place of birth. This is a fortunate placement so long as you are prepared to take risks, as they usually pay off for you. You are intensely curious and need to experience many different and diverse things. New experiences bring you great fulfilment. Allow yourself to radiate the joy that you feel within and don't try to convince those around you to see the world as you do. Just be a shining example of optimism and demonstrate a zest for life. You love travel of the mind or body. Teaching and learning give you pleasure. You'll be attracted to anything involving the expansion and awakening of consciousness.

Famous People

Rod Stewart, James Dean, Sigmund Freud, Michael Phelps, Bruno Mars, Billy Joel, Georges Pompidou, Jimmy Carter, David Cameron.

CAPRICORN

Your happiness comes from your determination to achieve your goals. You often lead the way for others and this can be a very good placement for luck in business and public affairs. Your greatest joy comes from observing your progress in life and seeing it take form and structure. You don't necessarily want things to come easily to you and you like to feel as though you have earnt your successes. You need to know that you can make a valuable contribution to society. This position may delay happiness until later in life. This is a sign of great depth and your joy is achieved after many years of focused effort. You know that what you achieve is not through good luck but rather from your own efforts and persistence. It is the awareness of your inner development that brings you your greatest joy. You love achievement, mastery, discipline, structure, organising and planning.

Famous People

Emily Dickinson, Victor Hugo, Winston Churchill, Anthony Hopkins, Richard Burton, Eva Perón, William Shatner, Gene Kelly, Johnny Carson.

AQUARIUS

Your happiness comes from making a tangible

contribution or creating an invention that is beneficial for everyone. You are able to raise money for charitable organisations. You could develop new cures in medicine. Others will seek you out for guidance and advice. You are fair and unbiased, and this is what attracts other people to you. You must never follow the paths of other people. You are original and creative and will come up with a new direction that is authentic to you. As soon as you accept that you are different and that your ideas are unique, you will feel much happier. Your joy is not only for yourself but for the good of all. You show others that they can celebrate their individuality. You love new ideas, the imagination, philanthropy, technology, science, the future, diversity and new inventions.

Famous People

Tina Turner, Maria Callas, Karl Marx, Frédéric Chopin, Simon Cowell, Whoopi Goldberg, Phil Collins, Maya Angelou, Dodi Fayed, Jude Law.

PISCES

You are naturally attuned to the spiritual side of life and you must concentrate on your higher ideals. This is where your true happiness lies. You will have a powerful magnetic and mysterious quality. You have a desire to bring about a more compassionate and loving world. You may have a strong interest in anything metaphysical, spiritual or esoteric and you get your greatest inspiration from tuning into the invisible forces. As you learn to go with the flow of life, to allow yourself to experience your emotions fully and not to avoid them or sweep them under the carpet, you will experience the oneness of everything and a deep sense of peace. You will probably be drawn to the helping professions. You love solitude, romance, poetry, being near water, charity, retreats, metaphysics and anything esoteric.

Famous People

Bob Marley, Johnny Depp, Liz Greene, Linda Goodman, Usher, Leonard Cohen, Eddie Murphy, Giacomo Casanova, Honoré de Balzac, Henry Miller.

CHAPTER FOUR

ASPECTS TO THE PART OF FORTUNE

As this is such a sensitive point in your chart, you are going to react very strongly when other people's planets touch it. You will also feel the important transits and progressions when they come around. Although the Part of Fortune is not a planet, it is an extremely powerful point in your chart because it is an amalgamation of the three most significant parts of your chart: your Sun, Moon and Ascendant.

For example, let's say you have your Part of Fortune in the fifth house conjunct the Moon. You will probably find joy in having a child. If your Part of Fortune is in the ninth house conjunct your Sun, you will probably love travelling and teaching and your good fortune comes from international connections.

Remember that, in astrology, there really is no such thing as a 'good' or a 'bad' aspect. It's just that some things take working on until you have accomplished the lessons that need to be learnt. Sometimes, this can take years to attain, with the feeling of taking one step forward and two steps back. However, often, when we have worked hard on something, it is much more gratifying than the things that come easily to us. There is a tendency not to appreciate the easy things and to value the things we have had to work for.

SQUARES TO THE PART OF FORTUNE

Don't be tempted to think that having a square to your Part of Fortune will deprive you of happiness. In fact, it is quite the opposite. A square creates tension, which will give you the

Where Is Your Part of Fortune?

impetus to initiate action and to bring about change. The more challenging the planets are that square the Part of Fortune, the more you will have to work at removing obstacles to your joy.

Easier planets forming square aspects to the Part of Fortune may bring you the fulfilment of your desires earlier in life or through an easier way. Let's say that you have beneficial squares to your Part of Fortune in the eleventh house. This would help you to actively seek out friendships, but, because those friendships come easily to you, you may not value them enough. If you have a square to your Part of Fortune in the fourth house, this will help you to have a harmonious family life, but you may take it for granted because it has come to you without much effort. You may want to be a concert pianist and, with squares to your tenth house Part of Fortune, you may put in the long hours practising in order to achieve the success you desire.

Squares create the discomfort to make you act. Whether the happiness you attain comes easily or with difficulty, whether it takes a short time or even a lifetime, it's very gratifying when you reach the fulfilment you seek and well worth the time and energy you expend in getting there.

TRINES TO THE PART OF FORTUNE

Planets that make trine aspects with your Part of Fortune bring outside events into your life that can lead you to happiness. It's important that you allow things to come to you rather than pursuing them, otherwise they will elude you. You need to learn how to go with the flow of people and experiences in your life and you will reach the fulfilment you seek without having to push for it.

Trines are not as easy as many people like to think. Challenging planets forming a trine to your Part of Fortune may put you through difficult experiences with others. However, these experiences will ultimately be the ones that lead you to your greatest happiness.

When the trines to your Part of Fortune are made by easier planets – for example, Venus, Jupiter or the Sun – it is very straightforward for you to attain your happiness. You will be very fortunate in that area of life in which your Part of Fortune falls in your chart. For example, if it's in your second house making a trine to Venus or Jupiter, you will be very fortunate with finances. Make sure you don't push your luck and you appreciate the fact that you are blessed in this area.

OPPOSITIONS TO THE PART OF FORTUNE

Planets in opposition to your Part of Fortune are best used for the benefit of others. They bring into balance your own needs with the needs of other people. By integrating these planets, you will feel more of a sense of connection and belonging to humanity. For example, if you have an opposition with your Part of Fortune in the fourth house with the Moon in the tenth, you will have to learn how to balance the emotional demands of your career with the needs of your family. Or you may have an opposition with your Part of Fortune in the sixth house with your Sun in the twelfth. This means that you need to learn how to balance the demands of work with a great inner need for solitude and peace.

CONJUNCTIONS TO THE PART OF FORTUNE

With conjunctions to your Part of Fortune, you need to learn how to use them in a positive way. The planet or planets making the conjunction will help to lead you to your happiness and joy.

Where Is Your Part of Fortune?

Sun Conjunct Part of Fortune

You have an optimistic nature, good self-esteem and strong vitality. This is often a sign of a long life but there would have to be other aspects in the chart to support this. You may earn money through your partner, through management or through anything connected with gold.

Moon Conjunct Part of Fortune

You like nurturing others, especially if your Moon is in a water or earth sign. You may earn your living through working with the public, music, acting, cooking, writing or anything connected with silver. This can indicate a happy emotional life so long as other aspects are supportive. It can lengthen your life.

Mercury Conjunct Part of Fortune

You love books, writing and talking, as well as communication in general. You may earn your living through writing, speaking, editing, teaching, accounting, health, computers, the internet or communication equipment.

Venus Conjunct Part of Fortune

You love beauty, art, luxury, anything sweet, harmony, elegance, romance and music. You may earn your living through jewellery, fine clothes, hair and skin products, perfumes, diamonds, gourmet food, music or art.

Mars Conjunct Part of Fortune

You love action, energy, competition, sport, fitness and making money. You may earn your living through fast cars, sports, sharp tools, surgery, aggressive sales, real estate, inventions or innovations.

Jupiter Conjunct Part of Fortune

You love teaching and learning. You may earn

your living through ships, planes, publishing, the media, producing or directing, charity, law, gambling, philanthropy, religion, academia or teaching.

Saturn Conjunct Part of Fortune

You enjoy discipline, hard work, deep study, intellectual concentration, responsibility, architecture, graphic art, building, gardening, medicine, mathematics and design. You may earn your living through architecture, science, medicine, construction, business, administration or politics.

Uranus Conjunct Part of Fortune

You like unusual things such as experimental music and art, new inventions, astrology, tarot, UFOs, space travel, anything that's high-tech, computers, radical ideas, extremes, gadgets, robots and artificial intelligence. You may earn your living through computers, computer software or games, inventions, electricity, mind toys and games, or aviation and flight.

Neptune Conjunct Part of Fortune

You love mystical things, the sea, music, escape, films, romance, dreams, poetry, photography and night life. You may earn your living in anything connected to photography, alcohol or mood-altering substances, oil, music, oceans, fish, videos, film, media, research, healing, psychic work or poetry.

Pluto Conjunct Part of Fortune

You enjoy intensity, power and emotional extremes. You have a strong will and are able to manifest whatever you desire. This is a great combination for politics or drama. You may earn your living through excavations, research, surgery, insurance, the nuclear industry, nuclear medicine or chemicals. This can indicate immense wealth if it is supported by the other aspects.

Where Is Your Part of Fortune?

No Aspects to the Part of Fortune

Don't panic if you don't have any aspects to your Part of Fortune, as this is quite common. If this is the case, then study the planet that is closest to your Part of Fortune. It will give you a clue as to how to reach your happiness. Don't forget that, not only do planets transit your Part of Fortune, but also people will come into your life whose planets connect with your Part of Fortune. As such, even without any natal aspects, there will be times when you experience its pleasure more acutely. For example, I have three very close friends who are all born on February 6th and I often wondered why. Then I learnt that their Sun is conjunct my Part of Fortune, so my interactions with them enhance my life in a positive and joyful way.

Keep in mind that the Part of Fortune appears in one house and one sign in your chart. This indicates the specific area in which you will be able to experience a deep sense of joy and fulfilment.

CHAPTER FIVE

FAMOUS PEOPLE'S PART OF FORTUNE

Examples of Famous People's Charts and the Part of Fortune

To illustrate the Part of Fortune in greater depth, I will examine some celebrity charts so that you can see how it plays out in their lives.

First House Part of Fortune

Madonna has her Part of Fortune in the first house in Virgo. She is someone who is very conscious and aware of the physical body, its presentation and its perfection. She is certainly 'one of a kind', which would correlate very well with the Part of Fortune in the first house. Even her name has a resonance with the sign Virgo. She achieved global recognition after the release of her second studio album, Like a Virgin, which is, interestingly, another link to the sign of her Ascendant and also the Part of Fortune. Virgo also rules service to others and Madonna is well known for her philanthropy and support, especially of children in third-world countries.

Second House Part of Fortune

Richard Branson's Part of Fortune is in the second house of money and finance. It's a wonderful illustration of a positive use of finance, entrepreneurialism, philanthropy and having clear values that are not only money-motivated but also directed towards helping others. Not surprisingly, his Part of Fortune is in Virgo, which indicates wanting to help others through his financial success. He is an English businessman best known for his Virgin Group of more than 400 companies.

Where Is Your Part of Fortune?

He was always entrepreneurial and started a magazine at the age of 16. When he was just 22 years old, he opened the chain of record stores known as Virgin Records. He is currently the fourth-richest citizen of the UK. He has certainly found good fortune with wealth and even owns a private island.

Ninth House Part of Fortune

Neil Armstrong has his Part of Fortune in the ninth house. This house rules long-distance travel, going to places that have never been seen or explored before, going beyond boundaries and seeing new worlds. This can be applied on a physical, emotional, mental or spiritual level. What could be a more apt placement for someone who was the first person to walk on the Moon? He publicly recalled his initial concerns about his Apollo 11 mission, and he said: "I was elated, ecstatic and extremely surprised that we were successful." He actually thought that it had just a 50% chance of success. Perhaps having the Part of Fortune in his ninth house helped him with his extraordinary achievement.

Part of Fortune in Taurus

Queen Elizabeth II has her Part of Fortune in Taurus. There is no doubt that she has immense wealth, despite the fact that her personal fortune has been the subject of speculation for many years. She does not have to worry about her finances and her physical needs are most surely being met. She has several residences – for example, Buckingham Palace, Windsor Castle, Sandringham House and Balmoral Castle – which, while not hers personally, are held in trust. She has full use of these beautiful places, where she entertains Heads of State, other royal personages and various VIPs. Taurus rules wealth and the Queen of England is an excellent example of this placement in her chart.

Where Is Your Part of Fortune?

Part of Fortune in Virgo

Mother Teresa epitomises the Part of Fortune in Virgo. She founded the Missionaries of Charity, which began as a small order with 13 members in Calcutta; by 2012, it had grown to more than 4,500 sisters and is active in 133 countries. They run orphanages, AIDS hospices and charity centres worldwide, and care for refugees, the blind, the disabled, the aged, alcoholics, the poor and homeless, and victims of floods, epidemics and famine. Virgo represents the Virgin and rules selfless love and service to others, and Mother Teresa showed this in an incredibly powerful way during her lifetime and she also leaves a powerful legacy. She received numerous honours, including the Nobel Peace Prize in 1979. She was also beatified in 2003.

Part of Fortune in Aquarius

Simon Cowell has his Part of Fortune in Aquarius.

Since Aquarius rules the individual, someone who doesn't compromise, who is unique and who sticks to his own opinions, Simon Cowell fits his Part of Fortune impeccably. As a judge on many talent shows, he is known for his blunt and often controversial criticisms, insults and wisecracks about contestants and their abilities. He is also known for combining activities in both the television and music industries, having promoted singles and records for various artists, including television personalities. Aquarius also rules humanitarianism and a desire to help others, and Cowell supports many charities, including a children's hospice, and is known for his financial help for many children's charities.

CHAPTER SIX

PART OF FORTUNE FROM A SOUL PERSPECTIVE

On the deepest level, the Part of Fortune shows an energetic frequency in your chart where you can derive perfect harmony.

For the day Part of Fortune, you are looking at your HEART energy.

For the night Part of Fortune, you are looking at your SOUL's vibration.

Those two points are very sensitive and highly attuned areas of your chart. Although they do not contain planets, tuning into their vibrational frequency can give you a great deal of information as to your life's purpose, your destiny and your ability to experience and access joy at the deepest level.

For the diurnal Part of Fortune, the Sun is on the Ascendant and we look to the placement of the Moon to find this sensitive point in your chart.

The questions this brings to light are:

If you were aligned perfectly with your real inner self and with your outer mask, what would that feel like?

If you were aligned perfectly with your real inner self and with your outer mask, what kind of emotional needs might you experience?

How can you tune in with your heart?

The Sun is your inner self and identity while the Ascendant is your outer self. When these

Where Is Your Part of Fortune?

are aligned, you have authenticity, realness and divinely inspired use of the will.

For the nocturnal Part of Fortune, the Moon is brought to the Ascendant and the point where the Sun falls shows the night Part of Fortune.

The question this point prompts is:

If your heart were aligned with your outer appearance, what would your identity look like? It's about learning to honour your feminine side and to be able to express it in the world.

You now have the basics with which to research and study your own Part of Fortune – both day and night – and to find out the best ways in which you can achieve abundance and prosperity in the mundane world, and contentment and deep joy in your inner world.

I hope this book has whetted your appetite to find

out more about your Part of Fortune and to see how you can constructively apply it to your life.

This is a topic I am continuing to research. If you have any comments or feedback, I'd be delighted to hear from you. You can email me on *barbaragoldsmith33@gmail.com*.

For further ways to contact me or keep up with my work, you can use the following platforms.

Facebook
www.facebook.com/barb.gold.50
Part of Fortune in Astrology Group

YouTube
www.youtube.com/user/barbaragoldsmith

Website
www.yourastrologysigns.com

Twitter
@barbaragoldsmit

REFERENCES

The Lot or Part of Fortune
by Robert Hand, 1996,
posted in Newsgroup Alt. Astrology

The Part of Fortune in Astrology
by Judith Hill, 1998

The Part of Fortune in Astrology
by Seth Thomas Miller, 2010

Karmic Astrology: Joy and the Part of Fortune
by Martin Schulman, 1978

Printed in Great Britain
by Amazon